10 Innovation Lessons through Short Stories

Contents

Idea generation

You need to be able to generate ideas freely without fear of judgment or criticism. this helps you learn new things in a fun and engaging way.

Explore to Learn

there was a young boy named Jack. Jack was always curious about the world around him and wanted to learn more about it. However, he often felt discouraged from asking too many questions or expressing his ideas freely. Jack's teacher noticed his eagerness to learn and encouraged him to explore his surroundings without any fear.

One day, Jack went on an adventure to explore the woods near his house. He found a small stream and followed it, which led him to an old tree with a hollow trunk. Jack thought to himself that it would be cool to have a treehouse in there. He started brainstorming different ideas: how to make the ladder to reach the top, how to design the inside, and how to make the lookout.

Jack built his treehouse with passion and excitement. Everyone who saw it admired Jack's creativity and hard work. His treehouse became the talk of the town, and Jack received recognition for his effort. From that day on, Jack realized that it was important to generate ideas freely without any fear of judgment. He is now more confident and curious than ever before and is always eager to learn new things.

Message: Learning how to generate ideas freely and creatively is an essential skill that will benefit you in the future. It helps develop critical thinking, problem-solving, and creativity, which will guide you throughout your adult life. So go ahead, be curious about the world around you, and explore! Who knows what adventure it may lead you to?

Problem-solving

You can develop the skill of problem-solving by learning to identify problems and come up with creative solutions. this skill will help you in the future.

the Problem-Solving Hero

In a faraway kingdom, there was a boy named Ben. Ben had always been fascinated with science and loved to invent things. One day, he found out that the kingdom was facing a problem. A dragon had attacked the castle and burned down the crops. The royal family had no solution to the problem, and the people were starving.

Ben decided that he wanted to help, and with his scientific mind, he identified the problem. He knew that the dragon was attracted to the red color, and that was why it attacked the kingdom. He came up with the idea of making a huge red flag to lure the dragon away from the kingdom.

Ben's idea worked, and the dragon followed the flag, leaving the kingdom in peace. The people cheered Ben, and the king rewarded him for his bravery and creativity.

From that day forward, Ben became known as the problem-solving hero. He continued to help the kingdom by finding creative solutions to their problems.

Message: Learning how to identify problems and come up with creative solutions is a critical skill that will help you in your future life. It develops critical thinking, problem-solving, and decision-making skills. So, do not be afraid to identify problems and think outside the box for creative solutions. You can be a problem-solving hero just like Ben!

Adaptability

Being adaptable in your thinking and willing to adjust ideas and approaches as needed is a valuable skill that will help you in your future life.

the Flexibility Master

there was a young girl named Lily. Lily loved playing soccer and was always focused and determined to win. One day, her team was playing in a tournament, and they were losing badly. Lily's coach suggested trying a different approach and changing their strategy.

At first, Lily was reluctant to change what she knew, but her coach reminded her that sometimes being flexible and willing to adjust is important. So Lily started coming up with new approaches to changing the game and using different soccer strategies.

Her team started winning with the new strategy just when it mattered the most. Lily realized that being adaptable in our thinking is essential, allowing us to come up with new ideas and solutions that we might not have considered before.

From that day on, Lily's willingness to adapt and adjust made her a stronger player and a better soccer team member.

Message: Being adaptable in your thinking and willing to adjust ideas and approaches as needed is a critical skill that will help you navigate changes and challenges you may face in life. It helps develop the ability to think on your feet and encourages creativity. So, always be willing to try new things, adjust when needed, and become an expert in flexibility, just like Lily.

Research

Encouraging you to research and gather information is a vital skill that can help you generate innovative ideas.

the Information Explorer

there was a young boy named Alex. Alex loved to create new things and often came up with innovative ideas. One day, he decided that he wanted to build a spaceship.

Alex knew he needed information and tools to succeed in building a spacecraft. So he began researching and gathering information on how rockets work, how to design a spacecraft, and what materials he needed to ensure it could get to space.

He spent hours reading books, watching videos, and talking to experts. He learned about every little detail he could and became a mini-expert in space technology.

Finally, after gathering all the information he needed, he started construction on his spaceship. His design was unique, and his knowledge helped him perfect every detail. Alex's spaceship was perfect and worked incredibly well, just like he had imagined!

Message: Encouraging you to research and gather information is a crucial skill that will help you succeed in the future. As you learn how to navigate the vast amount of information available to you, you will acquire the ability to make informed decisions. Being able to gather the right information and use it effectively can help you generate ideas and invent. So, be like Alex and become an information explorer who utilizes knowledge to create unique and innovative solutions.

Creativity

tapping into your creativity is an essential skill that can help you come up with new and unique ideas.

The Creative Genius

In a small town, there was a young girl named Amy. Amy was always dreaming up new and unique ideas. She loved to create new things and often found herself lost in her imagination.

One day, Amy saw her town struggling with waste management, litter all around, and plastic bags everywhere she went. She decided that she wanted to do something about it. After thinking for a while, Amy came up with an innovative solution to create a recycling program for garbage that even included a scheme for composting waste.

She used her creativity, and she drafted a plan to bring together the entire community to help reduce garbage creation and educate everyone on how to manage it. Her idea was embraced, and the entire town started supporting her.

With her hard work and unique ideas, the recycling program became a success, and it helped clean the town, with more people beginning to use reusable bags, bottles, and containers.

Message: Tapping into your creativity is a valuable skill that can help you come up with new and unique ideas to overcome challenges and innovatively solve problems. Encouraging your creativity will help you develop a unique approach to problem-solving and generate original solutions that can have a significant impact on the world. So, be like Amy, the creative genius, and use your imagination to contribute towards making the world a better place!

Collaboration

Working together and sharing your ideas can spark innovation and help you learn how to collaborate effectively.

the Innovation team

In a small village by the ocean, there was a group of young friends named tom, Jack, and Jane. One day, they decided that they wanted to build a boat, but they realized that they each had different skills.

Tom was great at drilling and hammering, Jack was good with saws and woodwork, and Jane was highly creative with drawing and designing.
Together, the friends realized that they could be an innovation team. They shared all their unique ideas, and they worked hard to make sure each person's skills could shine. As they worked on the project, they faced some challenges that were too difficult. But they all put their minds together, talked through their problems and ideas, and came up with unique solutions to each obstacle.

Finally, after many long hours of work, their boat was complete. Their collaboration enabled them to develop a unique and fascinating boat design that no one else had thought of!

Message: Encouraging you to work together and share your ideas can lead to innovation. Collaborating on ideas and working through challenges together can help you develop new and effective ways to solve problems. In the future, being able to work effectively as part of a team will be a crucial skill for you. So, be like tom, Jack, and Jane, the innovation team, and celebrate each other's strengths while working together to achieve greatness.

Risk-taking

Being willing to take risks and try new things is an important skill that can help you overcome your fears and learn new skills.

the Risk taker

there was a young boy named Max who was always scared to try new things. One day, his friend showed him a video of people doing stunts on skateboards. Max was amazed, and he wanted to try it out, but he was afraid of falling.

Max knew it would be a risk, but he decided he was going to try it. He even borrowed his friend's skateboard! As he stepped on the skateboard, his legs started to shake. He was unsure of himself, but he continued trying.

Max began to skate around clumsily, and before he knew it, he lost his balance and fell, but he did not give up. He continued practicing and taking risks, and soon he was able to perform the stunts he had seen in the video.

Max learned that even though he was scared, trying new things can lead to lots of fun and excitement, and most importantly, some lessons like falling and getting back up. Without trying, he would not have known, and he could not find his new loves or new passions.

Message: Being willing to take risks and try new things is an essential skill that can help you develop your confidence and grow as an individual. trying new things, such as sports, music, exploring new interests, or even meeting new people, can lead to new experiences, learning, and opportunities. So, be like Max, the risk-taker, and do not let fear hold you back from exploring new possibilities.

Resourcefulness

Being resourceful and using available resources can help you come up with innovative solutions to overcome challenges and problems.

the Resourceful Inventor

there was a young girl named Sarah. She loved creating new things and often invented gadgets in her free time. One day she came up with the idea to build a toy car, but she did not have any wheels to use.

Instead of giving up, Sarah decided to be resourceful and start looking for alternatives. She found some old CDs lying around, and she thought of using those as wheels.

She then found some old chopsticks and some cardboard. Sarah used these materials to build her toy car, using the CDs as wheels and attaching them to the cardboard frame with chopsticks to hold it all together. To her amazement, the car worked and glided smoothly across the floor. Her invention had come to life, and she was extremely proud of it!

Message: Being resourceful and using available resources can help you come up with innovative solutions to overcome challenges and problems. It encourages you to explore diverse ways of utilizing materials to create new things, enabling you to develop your problem-solving skills without relying solely on brand-new resources. This skill is valuable for the future as it enables you to maximize what you have and learn how to be sustainable. So, be like Sarah, the resourceful inventor, and continue to explore alternatives to tradition, discovering unique and creative solutions to any challenge you may encounter.

Reflection

Reflecting on the innovative process can help you understand what worked well and what you can improve upon for even better solutions.

the Reflective Innovator

There was a young boy named Alex who loved to create new things. One day, he decided to build a robot that could help with chores around the house. Alex spent days researching and gathering materials. He designed and built his robot all by himself.

When he finished the robot, he was extremely proud of his invention. But after using the robot for a few days, Alex realized that some parts needed more improvement. He noticed that the robot's arms were too short to pick up some items, and some of the parts used could be stronger to make the robot more durable.

Rather than being disappointed, Alex chose to reflect on the process. He thought about what he had learned throughout the process and how he could improve his robot. Alex made changes and improvements accordingly, which made his robot even better.

Message: Reflecting on the innovative process is essential because it enables you to identify what worked well and what you could improve upon. This helps you develop your critical thinking and problem-solving abilities as you seek solutions to enhance your inventions. Moreover, it teaches you to acknowledge imperfections and strive for improvement, even when outcomes do not meet your expectations, rather than giving up. Reflective innovators create better things, and this skill will serve you well in your future endeavors. So, be like Alex, the reflective innovator, and always reflect on your work to constructively improve.

Entrepreneurship

Encouraging you to think like entrepreneurs inspires you to consider how your innovative ideas can create value in the world and generate an impact.

The Young Entrepreneur

There was a young girl named Lily. She loved baking and had recently learned to prepare her grandmother's cookie recipe. Her family and friends loved them, and Lily thought to herself, "What if my cookies can be sold on the market?"

Lily decided to think like an entrepreneur. She started working on a business plan and, together with her parents, started selling cookies at the local farmer's market. They got a slot, and upon displaying her cookies for sampling, people loved them, and they started buying in bulk.
Lily realized that she could reinvest some money back into her business, expand her cookie-making business by adding more flavors and healthy options like gluten-free and vegan cookies, and even advertise online.

Through her entrepreneurial mindset, she realized that her ideas could impact the world, so she donated a portion of her profits to a charity that supports the homeless.

Message: Thinking as an entrepreneur encourages you to consider how innovative ideas can create value, impact society, and generate income. When you have an entrepreneurial mindset, you begin to think creatively and search for creative ways to launch or promote your innovative ideas to the world. It is not just about creating and innovating; it is about understanding how your ideas can contribute value to the world. These skills build confidence, financial literacy, and risk-taking, all of which are essential for success in the business world. So, follow in the footsteps of Lily, the young entrepreneur, and start exploring how your innovative ideas can create value for the world.